How To Get Answers Every Time You Pray®
As A Friend
By S. A. Polk

This is a work of nonfiction. No names have been changed, no character invented, no events fabricated.

Published by Interfaith University Press in partnership with AMC Consultants

Printed in the United States of America

Table of Contents

What is a Friend?

"And the Lord turned the captivity of Job, when he prayed for his friends: also the Lord gave Job twice as much as he had before." Job 42:10 (KJV)

We have come across many friends in our lives- some that were good friends; some "so call friends." Let's face it; we all want the best for our friends. Have you ever wanted to pray for a particular friend, but you did not know how? One thing about a true friend is that they will love you regardless. Love is a choice. Love is unconditional despite of another person's attitude, character, ways, or point of view. It is

2

consistent; at the same time, you have to choose wisely those you let into your heart.

The story of Job is about a man who almost lost everything. Initially, his friends were very encouraging and supportive. I am quite sure we all have experienced personality changes in our friends during difficult circumstances. So, we have Job, a righteous, and upstanding man whose circumstances change. Everything that Job loved was taken away from him, his children, animals, servants, crops; his wife even tells him to curse God, but Job refuses. Job's love and faithfulness to God was challenged by Satan. With all this is going on Job turns to his friends for support. As I mentioned before, friend's personalities can change. At the beginning of Job's trouble, his friends were with him, but their perspective of Job's character changes. Job's friends turned against him; they started criticizing and finding fault. You may have had similar situations with friends such as this. Despite what Job was going through and how his friends turned against him, Job prayed for his friends. His heart and love towards them compelled him to pray for them. Forgiveness is the key. This is a characteristic of Jesus. Thus, God spared his friends' lives and restored to Job twice what he had lost. An answered prayer.

Forgiveness is powerful. We have come across some friends that have offended us, vice versa. Even though circumstances may be different, but if we take the time to pray and forgive, all will be restored for you and your friends. Anytime that you are offended or have been done wrong, be careful how you react. **"We don't fight against flesh and blood but principalities, against powers, against the rulers of the darkness of this world, against spiritual wickedness in high places" Ephesians 6:12 (KJV).**

Instead of Job praying against his friends and reacting unreasonably, he prayed for them. As a result, God had blessed him and his friends. God holds us accountable for how we treat people. If you show mercy, you receive mercy (Matthew 5:7). Ephesians 4:32 says,

"And be ye kind one to another, tenderhearted, forgiving one another, even as God for Christ's sake hath forgiven you."

"Forbearing one another, and forgiving one another, if any man have quarrel against any: even as Christ forgave you, so also do ye." Colossians 3:13 (KJV)

"But if ye forgive not men their trespasses, neither will your Father forgive your trespasses."

Matthew 6:15 (KJV)

Do you know the biblical definition of the word friend? It seems we have lost the true meaning of the word "friend." Today we use words like "pal," "bestie," "fam," "partner," "ace boon," "homie," "ride or die," "roommate," "dawg" to call our friends. Let us look at what Jesus had to say.

"Henceforth I call you not servants; for the servant knoweth not what his lord doeth: but I have called you friends; for all things that I have heard of my Father I have made known unto you." John 15:15 (KJV)

The most commonly used word for *friend* in the Old Testament is *reeh,* which is translated to mean **"friend," "friendship," or "be friendly".** The Hebrew word comes from two root words meaning **"one who loves."** In Greek, the word friend is **philos (fee-los)** which means *a friend; someone dearly loved (prized) in a persona, intimate way; a trusted confidant, held dear* *in a close bond of personal affection.* The root word *(phil-) conveys experiential, personal affection.* **Phílos** *expresses experience-based love.* In the scripture above, Jesus is talking to His disciples before he was betrayed by Judas, (who was a friend). At this point, the disciples have been following Jesus for about three years. If you look closely at the above Scripture, there are two levels of friendship. The first level of friendship is a servant. In Greek, **servant** means **doulous (doo-los) a slave bond-slave, without any ownership rights of their own.** It is a description of believers who willingly live under Christ's authority as His devoted followers. In a servant stage, the Disciples did not know what was in Jesus' heart or what He must accomplish to unite mankind to our Father in Heaven. Jesus only told them what they were supposed to do. It is similar to those we call "friends", but we may call them here or there, do quick errands with them, but we do not necessarily tell them what is in our hearts. The disciples were tested with many trials and tribulations to prove themselves trustworthy enough to carry the gospel after Jesus ascended to Heaven left. As God was elevating Jesus, Jesus elevated His disciples who served Him faithfully to be *friends*.

The second level of friendship is to be called a *friend; this* implies that Jesus is able tell his disciples as much as he could bear what his Father "God" told Jesus to do. Similarly, today, this type of friendship means you can tell this person anything--- they have your best interest at heart and are willing to invest in what you do, whether it is with finances, words of encouragement, time. They are transparent, loyal, correct you when you are wrong, and make sacrifices for you to be a better person. Prayer to God for our friends shows the greatest love. Read John chapter 15 for yourself for a better understanding of friendship.

Walking In Agreement

"Assuredly I say unto you, whatsoever you bind on earth shall be bound in heaven and whatsoever ye shall loose on earth shall be loosed in heaven. Again say unto you that if two of you shall agree on earth as touching anything that they shall ask, it shall be done for them of my father which is in heaven." **Matt. 18:18-19 (KJV)**

Can two walk together, except they be agreed? Amos 3:3 (KJV)

To agree comes from the Greek word *sumphoneo* (soom-foe-neh-oh) from *sum together* and phoneo- *to sound*. **Sumphoneo** means *to sound together, to be in a* *symphony, to be in accord, to be in harmon*y. Metaphorically, the word means to agree together in prayer. Can you agree by yourself, yes, but prayer is more powerful when two or more people are in agreement.

"Again I say unto you. That if two of you shall agree on earth as touching any thing that they shall ask, it shall be done for them of my Father which is in heaven. For where two or three are gathered together in my name, there am I in the mist of them. Matthew 18:19-20 (KJV)

The next question is what are we agreeing about? What are we believing God for? Is it health, wisdom, direction etc.? Another question, what scriptures are we confessing in prayer? As we pray together with other believers in Christ, Christ's presence is in the midst of us! Hallelujah! I understand during these difficult times we may not be able to meet together like we want, but since we are in Christ Jesus it's our spirits' that connect us together as one in Jesus name. As we go further into the next chapters, we'll go more in depth on these matters. My Friend, we must agree on everything together!! Never forget you are never alone. When we pray together with the body of Christ for our friends, results manifest and God gets all the glory.

What Is Prayer?

Let's define the word *prayer* or *pra*y.

Pray, as explained by Jesus, means in the Greek **prosseuchomai** (pros-yoo-khom-ahee). The word is progressive, starting with the noun **euche**, a prayer to God that includes ***making a vow***.

The word expands to the verb ***euchomai***, a special term describing "an invocation, request or entreaty." Adding ***pros,*** in the direction of God, **prossechomai** becomes the most frequent word used for *prayer*.

It's how we are able to communicate with God in Jesus name.

Therefore I say unto you, What things soever ye desire when ye pray, believe that ye

receive them, and ye shall have them. And when ye stand in prayer forgive, if ye have ought against any: that your Father also which is in heaven may forgive you your trespases. Mark 11:24 (KJV)

When you stand in pray for your friends, make you hold no offense or grudge against your friend or anyone.

On the Day of Pentecost, they were all together with one accord, and God came down (Acts Chapter 2)!

Unity at work directed toward God for negative or positive will get God's attention. Now we have unity- that is, if you have been born again, you have the measure of unity that brings you into the family of God. The key is to learn from the Word of God how to work that unity for the positive, productive reasons God gave it to you! Unity is not enough being left alone; it must be activated in the direction toward God!

As you pray to God for your friends, ask do I have the right person praying with me? Is this person a born-again believer? Does this person have the same values as me? *For where two or three are gathered in My name, I am there in the mist of them (Matthew 18:20).* We will discuss this more in the next chapter.

What Is "IT!"

Now let's deal with <u>IT</u>! One reason many Christians praying for their friends have unanswered prayers has to do with the IT! Some are praying for IT, and IT does not come. Why? IT must be in unity with the body of Christ. For it to be loose from heaven, we must agree with a person on Earth. As a friend in the body of Christ, we must pray in the Holy Ghost because he knows the mind of God. The following process will get you anything you need (Philippians 4:19), want (Psalms 23), or desire from God (Psalms 37:4); for it is the Father's good pleasure to give you answers every time you pray!

1. ***Analyze the situation***- Find out what your friends' needs are, what their debts

are, what their sickness is, or what their fear is about. Do they need direction for a certain situation. James 4:3 says that we must ask God to help us know ourselves, so we are not asking amiss! Romans 8:26 says, ***"In the same way the Spirit [comes to us and] helps us in our weakness. We do not know what prayer to offer or how to offer it as we should, but the Spirit Himself [knows our need and at the right time] intercedes on our behalf with sighs and groanings too deep for words."***

2. ***Research God's Remedy***- Just as you would ask your pharmacist or doctor which

medication is best for a specific problem, ask the great Physician to show you in His written Word what the cure is. Ask God for His perspective. Then search the scriptures and pray the answer. If it's sickness that your friend is dealing with, search the scriptures for healing, depression search joy and so on. Pray the answer until you have allowed the Holy Spirit to convince you of the truth that Christ has redeemed you or your friend from the curse of the law (Galatians 3:13).

3. ***Ask, Seek, Knock***- Once you know the will of God based on scripture- not a prophet or any other person- but have found it in the Word of God, then He

hastens his Word to perform it (Matthew 7:7)! This scripture helped me to see that God is always concerned about my friends.

What is man, that thou art mindful of him? And the son of man, that thou visitest him? Psalms 8:4 (KJV)

One of the greatest secrets of asking and receiving is that of being **bold** to come to the throne of grace to ask of God your request. Remember, we are seated in Heavenly places and have a right to do this. Keep this mental picture in your mind. You are physically sitting on Jesus' lap, who is seated on the right hand of God, and as you are praying to God, by the power of the Holy Spirit in Jesus name; He is interceding to God about your concern for your friend. Boldness is the key. (Heb. 4:16) Whenever you pray to God and you are fearful it's an indication that your heart may not right with God, or you have a lack of trust in God.

4. **Partner**- Still no results... Call for backup!! Partners in the body of Christ. Remember unity is key. remember friend, other saints have conquered this level of negative force, and you have access to their faith through the power of agreement (James 5:14-16)! Notice the Bible says, *"call for the Elders."* There are

two principles here that should not be ignored:

1. *Elder-* means *older,* not necessarily in age, but maturity in the Lord!

An elder is mature spiritually and mentally in the area that you are struggling with. Warning: if you have a problem or weakness, a prayer partner with the same weakness is *not* going to build you up, for they have not developed themselves to the point that they are strong enough to bear your infirmity and theirs!

2. Remember that the binding and losing power is connected to the body of believers in Christ Jesus. Make it a rule

not to partner with anybody in prayer who is not firmly rooted in body of believers in Christ Jesus! (At least not to get your deliverance!) It is fine to pray with a person who is not in the body of believers in Christ Jesus who understands that the focus of the prayer is for their edification but remember, if you need strength, you must find strong prayer partners (Matthew 18:18-19). You may go as far as to say that you already have a prayer partner, but there is still a problem. In such a case, start at steps 1-4 and if all lines are clear, bring in another prayer partner and another and another until you have enough power in prayer to bind the strong man or negative force that is blocking the flow of your friend's blessing! Just make sure every prayer partner understands and has done the above things and can agree with you that this IT is God's will and He wants you to have IT. Start building your prayer partnership today!

5. *Praise and worship God in Faith and watch it manifest!*

6. *Separate from bad company, negative friends, bad teaching and preaching not in faith in God's total Word (I Corinthians 15:33 KJV).*

7. *If the enemy attacks you with doubt- do it again (Galatians 6:6 KJV).*

The bottom line is your IT must line up with your prayer partner's level of faith and the Father's will in Heaven. Well, how do we know the will of the Father. Pray the answer. Make sure that your IT is not built on lust or desiring something just because someone else it. Now, what is your IT?   Matthew 6:33 deals with seeking first righteousness, and He will commence to dropping it on you!! How do you seek the kingdom?

1. **Watch and pray for opportunities to sow-** finance, time, energy and, prayer into an anointed ministry that is spreading the Good

News of THE KINGDOM OF GOD! A ministry with VISION.

2. **Preach the Word**- Witness to friends and neighbors. Give away King James Bibles, good sound Christian books, text a scripture, and share words of encouragement on social media. Share a scripture that God puts on your heart. Share your testimony of how God brought you through a situation. Get the gospel out any way you can in the Spirit of God. (Pray about it!!)

3. **Put God first**- Resist pride and self-righteousness and the temptation to think that you know what is best for your friend. Simply get out of the way and let God show you the

need in prayer. You may go to the store and buy what you need, but God may have you in the store to buy your friend fruit, not knowing that her health issues are from lack of vitamins. Pray until you find out what God wants your friend to have because that is *their* need. Your family may require only a two-bedroom house, but to help your friend's family, they may need a five-bedroom home. Seek first the kingdom and His righteousness! It's time to get **IT** right because when you hunger and thirst to do right by helping others, you will be blessed and blessed and blessed. Well, should you run off and sow a financial seed to everything asking and moving or looking like the kingdom? No!! Would you sow peas one or two or three to a field? No!! Because you would have to go to two or three different locations just to get started on a pot!! The bottom line is to sow where:

1. God leads,

2. The ground is good,

3. The Gospel is being preached,

4. Souls are being saved, and

5. Christians are edified.

Do all of this under the anointing or the witness of the Holy Spirit! Pray. God will direct your path. What is **IT**? Let's touch and agree, and it shall be done according to God's will.

It's God's Will To Pray For Our Friends

"Rejoice evermore. Pray continually without ceasing. In everything give thanks: for this is the will of God in Christ Jesus concerning you."

1 Thessalonians 5:16 (KJV)

We have already established that God's Word is His will. Consistency is key!! If you genuinely want to get answers every time you pray for your friend and be a blessing, you must allow God to speak to your heart about your friend's need and back it up with Scripture. Scripture that has been revealed from the Word of God and put your faith in God. That is right, the moment God makes a word alive in your spirit, you have faith. *Now!*

Hebrews 11:1 says, "*Now faith is the substance of things hoped for, the evidence of things not seen.*"

Romans 10:17 tells us, *faith comes by hearing and hearing by the Word of God.*

It is Gods' will that we pray for our friends. 1 Timothy 2:4 says, "*Who will have all men to be saved, and to come unto the knowledge of the truth.* God invites you to pray for all of your friend's needs and wants. Don't limit God or His promises. Many men in the Bible prayed for their friends. Let's take a look at the results when they prayed for their friends.

In 2 Kings 6:17, we read about Elisha praying for his servant.   It is God's will that we pray for our friends. In this story, the servant was in fear of the enemy. Elisha prayed:

"Lord, I pray thee, open his eyes, that he may see. And the Lord opened the eyes of the young man; and he saw: and behold, the mountain was full of horses and chariots of fire round about Elisha."

A prayer answered. There was a war going on between Syria and Israel. The Syrians tried to surround Elisha, the Prophet. His servant feared because in the natural matter they were outnumbered, but God and His army of angels were with them in the spirit realm as Elishia prayed and asked God to open his servant's eyes in the spirit, to see that there was more with them than their enemy and when God opened the servant's eyes, he saw. An answered prayer.

As a friend, your faith maybe on a different level. Remember, if you want to come up in life or get answers every time you pray, it will take someone who is higher or more spiritually mature than you to bring you up. The same thing goes for prayer partners, as I mentioned earlier.

Another example of a friend praying for a friend Abraham and Lot. Although they were family, we can equate their relationship to a friendship. Abraham desired to follow God's way, but Lot desired to follow worldly ways. Abraham prayed that God would spare the lives of Lot and his family before God destroyed Sodom in Gomorrah (Genesis 18:16-33). God answered Abraham's prayer when He sent angels to escort Lot and his family to the mountains. An answered prayer. All were spared except the wife, who disobeyed and looked back.

Friendship Covenants

From the beginning, God is revealed as the covenant maker. The basic meaning of *"covenant"* in the Bible is summed up in Jeremiah chapter 31, verse 33: *"I will be their God; and they will be my people."* God enters into a special covenant with men and women. He commits Himself to protect His people, and in return, He expects obedience from them. Most covenants in the Bible are between God and men. There are also "man to man" covenants in the Old Testament. The Bible itself is arranged into two major "covenants"-the Old and the New. They are more often called the Old and New Testaments (which means the same thing). The Old Covenant is the one made with Moses on Mt. Sinai when the

Ten Commandments were given to God's people as the basic rules for living. This covenant forms the basis for Israel's religion. God and Moses' covenant was so tight that Moses spoke to God face to face; like you would with a friend. *"And the* ***Lord spake unto Moses face to face, as a man speaketh unto his friend."*** **Exodus (33:11 KJV)**

Moses spoke with God freely, without a doubt. Every time there was an issue, or a concern Moses had with the people or himself, he would always consult with God in the mountains. The one-on-one intimate conversations that drew Moses and God together that nothing could separate their love for each other. It was God's way of revealing a character of mercy, love, and kindness. Whenever Moses spoke with God, he always had an answered for the people and no doubt that some of them were his friends.

Before Moses, God made covenants with Noah and Abraham. The covenant made with Noah after the flood was God's general covenant with all people. Then there is the covenant God made with Abraham. Abraham is called the Friend of God.

"And the scripture was fulfilled which saidth, Abraham believed God, and it was imputed unto him for righteousness and he was called Friend of God." Ye see then how that by works a man is justified, and not by faith alone. James 2:23-24

The Scripture above refers to Abraham, who was first a servant of God but by Abraham's faith and obedience in his times of testing, he elevated to Friend of God.

God promised that his descendants would have a land of their own, and he urged them to share their blessings with the other nations of the earth. This is God's covenant with His special people, renewed in the covenant with Moses at Mt. Sinai.

Another Old Testament example of a covenant is the one made between Ruth and Naomi. These two women from different backgrounds become covenant friends. Ruth, a Moabitess, agrees to follow her mother-in-law back to her homeland and serve the God of Israel.

She came from a history of adulators. Ruth vowed to stick with her mother in law and friend, Naomi; *"And Ruth said, Intreat me not to leave thee, or depart from following after thee: for whither thou goest, I will go: and where thou lodgest, I will lodge: thy people shall be my people, and thy God my God: Where thou diest, will I die, and there will I be buried: the Lord do so to me and more also, if ought but death part thee and me." Ruth 1:16 (KJV)*

God honored her vow and made sure that both she and Naomi's need Ruth and were meet. By Ruth joining together in covenant friendship with Naomi, she ended up in the linage of Christ. Ruth found her purpose when she partnered with

Naomi. Many of our friends are searching for a purpose, which is to be conformed to the image of Christ (Romans 8:29). We can pray that God shows us whom to covenant with and that they understand their purpose in His Son Jesus.

The New Testament writers show that the New Covenant between God and men, to which the Old Testament looks forward, rests on the death of Jesus. Jesus Himself said, *"this cup of the New Covenant, sealed with My blood."* The Book of Hebrews compares the Old and New Covenants. The New Covenant offers something that the Old could never secure- release from the power of sin and the freedom to obey God. Here are more Scripture references on covenant; Exodus 19:6; 20:1-7; Genesis 9:1-17; 12:1-3; 15:17-21;

Jeremiah 31:31-34; I Corinthians 11:25; Hebrews 8:13; 10:4. We are no longer under the old covenant. My Friend we are in Christ Jesus who said,

"A new commandant I give unto you. That ye love one another; as I have loved you, that ye also love one another. By this shall all men know that ye are my disciples, if ye have love one to another. John 13:34-35 (KJV)

Impartation

What is impartation? To give, share, distribute, grant. The word implies **liberality** or **generosity**. Paul says it like this,

"For I long to see you, that I may impart unto you some spiritual gift, that ye may be established." Romans 1:11 (KJV)

When you come in partnership with the body of Christ, the spiritual gifts that they have are imparted to you. There strengths become your strengths. Let's look at David and Jonathan. "Now it came about when he had finished talking to Saul, that the soul of David and Jonathan were knit together, and he loved him as himself and Saul took him that day and did not let him return to his father's house. Then Jonathan made a covenant with David because he loved him as himself. And Jonathan stripped himself of the robe that was on him and gave it to David, with his armor, including his sword and his bow and his belt (I Samuel 18:1-4 NASV).

Impartation! What a covenant between two God-fearing men. They became unified in agreement. To the degree that Jonathan took down his defense and joined himself to David. He took his armor off, thus opening himself up to receive whatever David would return to him. David returned love. The armor was the token of exchange, which was common among covenant makers in the Bible. God gives protection and provision because we are now friends of God. We are to respond in loving obedience. In giving David his royal robe, his armor and sword, his bow, and belt, Jonathan was giving to David his authority of succession to his father's throne. As you see, it is important to be led by God to direct you, and He will show you what to impart to your friends.

He answered and saidth unto them, He that hath two coats, let him impart to him that hath none; and he that hath meat, let him do likewise. (Luke 3:11 KJV); to encourage people to give with cheerful outflow (Romans 12:8); and urge workers to labor with industry, to give to him who has a need (Ephesians 4:28).

Ephesians 4:7-8 says, "But unto every one of us is given grace according to the measure of the gift of Christ. Wherefore he saith, "When he ascended up on high, he led captivity captive, and gave gifts unto men." Therefore, every Christian has a gift in God. Verse (12) says, "...for the work of the ministry, for the edifying of the Body of Christ."

Writing to the body of believers in Christ Jesus at Rome, Paul says... "For I long to see you, that I may **impart** unto you some spiritual gift, to the end that ye may be established" (Romans 1:11). Here, to impart means simply "to give over and to share." It means to convey from one person to another. The apostle Paul had the desire to impart to the saints some spiritual gift or spiritual help.

Spiritual impartations are given to help us fulfill the will of God for our lives. This is part of the equipping. We are equipped to do the work of the ministry through impartation. We are more equipped to get answers every time we pray for our friends when we are connected to the body of Christ through believers in Christ Jesus. The result is an *establishment*. The New English Bible says, "to make you strong." The Twentieth Century New Testament says, *"and so give you fresh strength."* Thus, the believer is equipped with fresh strength as a result of impartation.

Impartation will often come through association. In this way, there will be a transference of anointing from or to the people you associate with. We can receive through impartation from the ministries we submit to and associate with.

There are certain people whom I believe the Lord has destined you to partner within the Spirit. They will have the spiritual deposits you need. It is not the will of God that we lack any necessary gift, information, materials, or anointing (in the manifestation of the Holy Spirit). He has given us the means to obtain all we need. He is ready and willing to equip us with all the grace we need to complete our commission to preach the gospel to all nations, make disciples of men and pray for our friends'.

If you see no results when you are praying for your friend, it is not God's fault. It is important to associate with strong body of believers in Christ

Jesus. If you associate yourself with weakness, you will become weak. If you associate with strength, you will become strong. You will become like the people you associate with. Do not allow yourself to become weak by linking up with the wrong kind of people. *"And God wrought special miracles by the hands of Paul; So that from his body were brought unto the sick handkerchief's or aprons, and the disease departed from them, and evil spirits went out of them"* (Acts 19:11-12). Once again, an object was exchanged (**Paul's materials**); as a point of contact (**tokens of the covenant**) to the other person involved in the impartation. What a Mighty God we serve!

A Prayer for Salvation for Your Friends

Philippians 4:6 says, *"Be careful for nothing; but in everything by prayer and supplication with thanksgiving let your request be made known unto God."*

Everything that concerns you or your friends take it into prayer. Don't be anxious for anything because prayer is the remedy for worry. There are three expressions or prayer;

1. Prayer- generally used or communication with God: a form of worship

2. Supplication- an intense form of prayer; a specific request or a specific need

3. Thanksgiving- a form of prayer from a heart of gratitude

God is our God of Peace, who calms all troubling situations and concerns we may have for our friends.

Most times, as a friend, we do not know how to pray for our friends. That is why we put our trust in Jesus by the power of the Holy Spirit to lead us. Romans 8:26 says, **"Likewise the Spirit also helpth our infirmities: for we know not what we should pray for as we ought: but the Sprit itself maketh intercession for us with groanings which cannot be uttered."**

Pray the prayer below for your friends:

Our Heavenly Father in the power of your Holy Spirit in the name of Jesus I humbly come to you interceding for my friend today. For you know their need even before I speak. For you said in your word that you desire for all men to be saved in 1 Timothy 2:4. Your word says that every knee shall bow, and every tongue shall confess that Jesus Christ is Lord. Father God help my friends admit that they are as sinner and that Jesus your Son died on the cross for their sins and you raised Him from the dead. Purify their hearts and renew a right spirit in them according to your word in Psalms 51. Father we ask that you fill them with your Holy Spirit and joy.

Clap your hands and shout for joy for your friend's salvation!!

Prayer for Protection for Our Friends

 God is always concerned about us; it is according to His Word

"The Lord will perfect that which concerneth me:" Psalms 138:8 (KJV)

"What is man, that thou art mindful of him? And the son of man, that thou visitest him?"

Psalm 8:4 (KJV)

God will even come down from Heaven to see about you. Remember friend, we don't fight against flesh and blood, but we fight against principalities, against power, against the rulers of darkness of this world, against spiritual wickedness in high places.

Let's pray, Our Heavenly Father by the power of your Holy Ghost and in the name of Jesus. I know you are strong and mighty in battle. You are our shield and defense. I bring my friend (name) before you concerning (his or her) safety. Every time I pray, you hear, and answer me. For you said in your word those that dwell in your secret place abides under you. I plead the blood of Jesus over (friend name) life, mind, body, and soul. I bind the spirit of sickness and disease! I bind the spirit of poverty and lack. I bind Satan, his plans, distractions, negative words, and traps that he has set against (friend name) that it stops NOW IN JESUS NAME. Any tongue that rises against (friend name) is condemned and shown to be in the wrong. For *your Word says that my enemies may come up*

against (friend name) one way but flee seven

ways. Your name will be glorified because

delivered (him or her) out of the hands of the

enemy. I release your Holy angels to surround

(him/her) right now . In Jesus name release your

anointing of peace, love, and joy in Jesus name.

Prayer reference: Psalm 91; Ephesians 6:11; Psalm 32:7; Psalm 46:1; Deuteronomy 31:6; Hebrews 13:6; Isaiah 54:17; Psalm 3; Psalm 16:8

A Prayer for Revival

Waves of revival swept around the world in the 20th Century. Today, the five largest body of believers in Christ Jesus in the world are Spirit-filled and growing daily. Pentecostals are increasing in great numbers as worldwide revival brings the life of God to the body of believers in Christ Jesus and to all mankind. The Hebrew word for revive is **chayah** which means *to live, have life, remain alive, sustain life, nourish, and preserve life, live prosperously, live forever, be quickened, be alive, be restored to life and health.* According to that definition, revival is not just a one-time shot of life. Revival is continual nourishment, preservation, quickening, and restoration to life. Revival begins when people return to God. It breaks forth from intercessory prayer and continues when people repent and no longer tolerate sin in their lives.

After Jesus ascended to heaven, the disciples returned to the upper room and continued in daily prayer, in one accord, and one place. Then, at the appointed time, the Holy Spirit burst onto the scene with the sound of a mighty rushing wind. Peter and the others received God's long-awaited promise of the Holy Spirit's anointing. Acts 2:17-19 repeats the prophecy of Joel, *"And it shall come to pass in the last days, says God, "And it shall come to pass in the last days, says God, That I will pour out my spirit in those days, And they shall prophesy... I will show wonders in heaven above and signs in the earth beneath..."* (New King James Version).

As they moved out into the streets from the upper room, men from every part of the world saw and heard something different. Peter's great sermon preached under God's anointing, brought understanding, the conviction of sin and the life of God to those who heard and responded in faith. Prayer, the anointed preaching of the Word, and a supernatural move of God all working together brought revival-God's life-giving power. Oh, what a time to live in! Destruction, a pandemic and despair may be on the one hand, but revival and miracles are on the other. Revival is spontaneous and ongoing. It happens when the Spirit of God moves among the people. God never intended for the Pentecostal revival to stop. That is why it is important to be ready and available as God moves and pours His Spirit. He can minister life at any moment, to one or a multitude, to a person in a barren wilderness, or to many people in a crowded city.

Revival happens whenever the Word of God prevails. Miracles, signs, and wonders happen wherever the Word of God prevails. Hearts and lives are changed wherever the Word of God prevails. The Bible says ...*God working with them and confirming His word with signs following* (Mark 16:20).

Look in the Word of God, which is life to them; revival will come and remain. Revival will become an ongoing way of life. As you set yourself in agreement with God's will for revival, pray the following prayer or one similar, expecting God to move in your friend's life.

"*Father God because you care for my friends and want all mankind to have life. You desire revival. Your revival brings life and nourishment, preservation, and restoration. Thank you for sending Jesus to give us Your abundant life Lord, start a revival in me first. I am Your friend and I place my friends in position to receive revival. They feed on the Scriptures as a sheep feeds in* green pastures, because Your words are life to them.

Holy Spirit of God, You raised Jesus from the dead and You dwell in (friend name). So, I humble ask that You would energize (friend name) spirit, restore their soul, and rejuvenate their mortal body. I ask you to renew their mind with Your Word. In their innermost being is a well of living water and they are revived! Revival not only is life to me, but life to everyone who calls on the Name of the Lord. Therefore, I intercede on behalf of (friend name). I call upon You as the God of Abraham, Isaac, and Jacob I call upon the mighty Name of Jesus. (friend name) needs life, Lord! (friend name) needs revival because in You is life forever more. our out Your Spirit on all flesh.

I speak and sow seeds of revival everywhere I go. I send forth angels to reap the harvest of revival all over the world. I put my hand to the sickle to reap the rich harvest of revival in my home, my community, my friends, in the marketplace, on the job, in my country and in all the world. Pour Yourself out on my friends. Lord of the harvest, send forth laborers, positioning them in strategic places to minister as You pour out Your Spirit on all flesh. Almighty God, show Yourself mighty and strong with signs and wonders. Holy Spirit breathe on all the of my friends in the world. I pray this in the Name above all names, Jesus. Amen."

Almighty God, show Yourself mighty and strong with signs and wonders. Holy Spirit breathe on all the of my friends in the world.   I pray this in the

Name above all names, in Jesus Name.   Amen."

Prayer references: John 3:16-17, 10:10; Proverbs 4:20-22; John 6:63; Romans 8:11; Ephesians 4:23-24; Colossians 3:10; John 4:14, 7:38; Matthew 13:39, 9:38; II Chronicles 16:9; Romans 15:19

Understanding Redemption

God can establish us in the faith according to the redemption plan that had been hidden over the ages. After the Fall in the Garden of Eden, God spoke and outlined the plan. What He laid down, put Satan out of business completely. Praise God! He has commanded that the plan of redemption be revealed to His people by His Word. This outline will help you, step by step, understand the reality of it and prevent Satan from lording over you and your friends.

1. **The Plan of Redemption called for an Incarnation** (The Union of Divinity with Humanity in Jesus Christ).

Man was the key figure in the Fall. Therefore, it took a man, Jesus, to be the key figure in man's redemption. When we were born into this world, ruled by Satan, we did not naturally know God. Therefore, the incarnation's objective is that men may be given the right to become sons of God by receiving the nature of God (John 1:12-13; II Peter 1:3-4).

2. **Redemption Comes From Knowledge.**

God's divine power has already provided everything that pertains to life and godliness. You can escape from the corruption in the world and partake of the divine nature of God, and you can have peace and grace multiplied to you through the knowledge of God and of Jesus our Lord (I

Peter 1:1-4).   It' is there for you!   But this revelation knowledge is not sensed knowledge, doctrine, philosophies, and creeds.   It is the reality, and full truth of the Word of God revealed by the Holy Spirit (James 3:13-18).

Revelation knowledge is literally knowledge brought to you by revelation!

3. **Satan's Lordship Has Been Broken.**

Revelation 12:11 tells us that the believers are overcome by the blood of the lamb and by the word of their testimony, or confession. Confession brings possession. Boldly confess,

For yourself, *"I am an overcomer by the blood of the Lamb and by the word of my testimony*.

I am redeemed from the lordship of Satan. I can stop his assignments every time."

For your friend, *"(friend's name) is an overcomer by the blood of the Lamb and by the word of my testimony. (Friend's name) is redeemed from the lordship of Satan. (He or she) can stop his assignments every time."*

(II Corinthians 10:4; James 4:7). Satan is not the head of the body of believers in Christ Jesus. Jesus is the head of the body of believers in Christ Jesus (Ephesians 4:15-16, 5:23; Colossians 1:18, 2:10). Satan has no rule over you or your friends. Hallelujah!

4. **You and Your Friends Are Bought with A Price.**

I Corinthians 6:19-20 tells us we are the temple of the Holy Spirit, which is received from God. This means that we do not own ourselves, neither do our friends. We were bought with a price paid through the plan of redemption. Because of that, we should glorify God in our bodies and spirits.

5. **God's Response.**

When you begin to take your place and assume your rights and privileges in Christ, God begins to respond to you. The Word gives us our inheritance (Acts 20:32; Colossians 1:12). As you study the scriptures in this outline, our prayer is that you come to the full knowledge of who you are in Christ, especially in light of the redemption plan. Once you know who you are in Christ, put your trust in Him then you will see and know how to pray for your friends. God will bless you! Amen!

The Power of Confession

Words are spiritual; they carry power. The words we speak are of vital importance not only to our lives but our friend's life as well. Jesus said, *"I say unto you, that every idle word that men shall speak, they shall give account thereof in the day of judgment. For by thy words thou shalt be justified, and by thy words thou shalt be condemned"* (Matthew 12:36-37). Life and death are in the power of your tongue. You have the ability to speak life for your friends.

When God created the human race, he placed in us the special ability to choose our own words and speak them forth at will. That ability makes the human being different from all other creatures, even the angels. Angels can speak, but they can only speak the words God tells them to speak. They act, but only by the command of God.

Man's unique ability to choose and speak words has become a key factor in developing of the human race. Proverbs 12:14 tells us that we shall be satisfied with good by the fruit of our mouths. In Matthew 12:34, Jesus said, "*...out of the abundance of the heart the mouth speaketh.*"

If we are not enjoying the reality of God's Word, it is because our confession has us bound. Confessing God's Word is not lying, for we must realize that we are not trying to get God to do anything. God cannot lie and he is not a respecter of persons. The benefits God has given us, and our friends are in His Word are ours already, and

Satan is trying to steal them! Satan's mission is to kill, steal, and destroy. (John 10:10)

So, confessions are not lies; they are a statement of the truth of God's Word. If you did not know, Jesus bore your sickness and disease and told someone you were healed because of your own merits; then you would be lying. But, to tell someone that your friend is healed because the Bible says, *"by His stripes you were healed,"* is speaking the truth that Jesus has already redeemed them from the curse of the law (Deuteronomy 28; Galatians 3:13).

Here are five basic confessions for you and your friends to use so that you can enjoy all that God has for you and your friends:

1. **Jesus is My Lord.** Philippians 2:9-11

"I confess the complete lordship of Jesus Christ. Jesus is Lord overall and He has given me authority. As I confess Him, His Word and His Name, and resist Satan in His Name, Satan must bow His knee."

As you confess for your friends, "I confess the complete lordship of Jesus Christ over (friend's name). Jesus is Lord overall and He has given (he or she) authority. As I confess Him, His Word and His Name, and resist Satan in His Name, Satan must bow His knee."

2. **I Do Not Have A Care.** I Peter 5:7; Psalms 37:23-24

"I cast all my care on Jesus because He cares for me. He upholds me as He guides my steps."

As you confess for your friends, "I cast all (friend's name) cares on Jesus because He cares for them. He upholds them as He guides their steps."

3. **I Do Not Want.** Psalms 23:1; Philippians 4:19

"The Lord is my Shepherd. I shall not want. For my God supplies all my need according to His riches in glory by Christ Jesus.

As you confess for your friends, "The Lord is (friend's name) Shepherd. (He or She) shall not want. For my God supplies all (his or her) need according to His riches in glory by Christ Jesus."

4. **Your Friends are Free From Sin, Sickness, Sorrow, Grief and Fear.** Isaiah 53:3-5; Matthew 8:17; I Peter 2:24

"Every sin, sickness, disease, sorrow and grief was laid on Jesus so that I could be free from them. Therefore, today I am forgiven, healed, healthy and well. I live in divine health."

As you confess for your friend, "Every sin, sickness, disease, sorrow and grief was laid on Jesus so that (friend's name) could be free from them. Therefore, today (friend's name) is forgiven, healed, healthy and well. (Friend's name) lives in divine health."

5. **Jesus is made unto us Wisdom, Righteousness, Sanctification and Redemption.** I Corinthians 1:30; Colossians 2:10

"I confess that Jesus is my wisdom, righteousness, sanctification, and redemption. Only in Him am I entirely complete."

As you confess for your friend, *"I confess that Jesus is (friend's name) wisdom, righteousness, sanctification, and redemption. Only in Him (she or he is) entirely complete."*

Continue to believe God to change your friend's circumstances by filling your heart with the Word of God for your friends. Teach them to make these confess too. Confess these truths and other Scriptures so that the words that come out of your mouth are life-changing words. Let your word be God's word!

YOUR OPPORTUNITY TO PARTNER

We see that partnership is indeed dynamic. However, partnership is not a one-sided relationship. As the Apostle Paul said, "*I thank my God upon every remembrance of you... For your fellowship in the gospel from the first day until now... because I have you in my heart; In as much as both in my bonds, and in the defense and confirmation of the gospel, ye are all partakers of my grace* (Philippians 1:3, 5,7)." Paul was saying, "I have you in my heart, I'm praying for you and I'm not going to let you fail!" His partners had become a major part of his ministry. They fought alongside him in prayer, they ministered to his needs and provided for other ministers that he sent to help build them spiritually. This is how partnership works.

Our Partners have a significant role in the mission. God provides for us through ministry through prayers, words of encouragement and support, and through their giving to what God is doing through us. Moreover, every day, we see and hear of the great rewards we are receiving through the mission and as well as our partners. If God is directing you to become a Partner, or if you are already a Partner, press in to get a revelation of God's will for you and to pray for our friends, and then get ready for the adventure and rewards that come when you release the power of partnership in your life.

The Blessing of Sowing Seeds

"And he...took the five loaves, and two fishes, and looking up toward heaven he blessed, and brake, and gave the loaves to his disciples, and the disciples to the multitude. And they did all eat and were filled: and they took up of the fragments that remained twelve baskets full. And they that had eaten were about five thousand men beside women and children" (Matthew 14:19-21).

Sowing into this mission helps better the lives of many people. We reach friends all over the globe through the principle of the twice sown seed.

When you give, 10 percent of every gift is given to purchase more books as a free gift to be given to those who desire to pray for their friends and a closer relationship with Christ. We are reaching greater numbers of friends through partnership with us than any of us could reach on our own-people who have no other way to hear the good news.

You enable us to put legs to our prayers by putting substance into our hands to be effective soldiers of the cross. As a result, you will share the reward of this harvest someday!   Lives are changed Eternally.   Blessings overflow to the giver and everything they put their hands to do.

A PARTNER............

One who shares responsibility in some common activity with another individual or group.

Our Part is to...

☐Pray on a daily basis that God's Blessing be upon you

☐ Study and diligently seek the Word of God

☐ Share words of encouragement and teaching letters from time to time

☐Offer from time to time, a special gift for your spiritual edification and growth.

Your Part is to...

☐ Pray for us always

☐ Support and attend all meetings

☐Support with your time, talent and treasure as the Lord shall direct

☐Always share your testimony and encouraging words

S. A. Polk, I want to access How To Get Answers Every Time You Pray® As a Friend Partnership!

My Name is:

_____

My Address is:

_____

_____

Phone: _____ Age: _____

M _____   F _____

I am writing my prayer request on this form.

Enclosed is my love gift of
$_____.

I am pledging ___ $7 ___$10   ___$20 ___$100

___$500   ___Other $_____ per month to help you

accomplish the vision of winning the lost and

encouraging the saints through the Word of God!

_____,
Signature

Prayer
Request_____

_____

Shonbooks.com

PRAYER FOR OUR PARTNERS

Father, in the Name of Jesus, we pray to you on behalf of our all of our partners, who pray for us, support us, sow financially, and always uplift us with the words that they speak.

Father, we thank you for our partners and for their service and dedication to serve. Thank you that they bring forth the fruit of the Spirit: love, joy, peace, longsuffering, gentleness, goodness, faith, meekness, and temperance.

Father, thank you that our partners are good ground, that understand our vision and understand it, and that the Word bears fruit in their lives. They are like trees planted by rivers of water that bring forth fruit in its season. Their leaf shall not wither, and whatever they do shall prosper.

From the first day we heard of our partners, we have not stopped praying for them. Give them wise minds and spirits attuned to his will, and so acquire a thorough understanding of the ways in which God works. Our partners are merciful as our Father is merciful. They will judge only as they want to be judged. They do not condemn, and they are not condemned. Our partners forgive others, and people forgive them. They give, and men will give to them- yes, good measure, pressed down, shaken together, running over will they pour into their laps for whatever measure used with other people, they will use in their dealings with them.

Father, we ask you to bless our partners with all spiritual blessings in heavenly places that goodwill might come to them. They are generous and lend freely. They conduct their affairs with justice. Lord, Your Word says that surely, they will never be shaken. They are righteous women who will be remembered forever. They will have no fear of bad news; their hearts are steadfast, trusting in you.

Lord, we ask that your plans be fulfilled in their lives, and we thank you for your mercies on their behalf. In Jesus' name, we pray. Amen.

Colossians 1:9 Psalm 112:5-9; Jeremiah 29:11

Scriptures on Friends

1. Job 42:10 (KJV)

And the Lord turned the captivity of Job, when he prayed for his friends: also the Lord gave Job twice as much as he had before.

2. John 15:15 (KJV)

Henceforth I call you not servants; for the servant knoweth not what his lord doeth: but I have called you friends; for all things that I have heard of my Father I have made known unto you.

3. James 2:23 (KJV)

And the scripture was fulfilled which saith, Abraham believed God, and it was imputed unto him for righteous: and he was called the Friend of God.

4. Exodus 33:11 (KJV)

And the Lord spake unto Moses face to face, as a man speaketh unto his friend. And he turned again into the camp: but his servant Joshua the son of Nun, a

*young man, departed not out of the
tabernacle.*

5. Proverbs 17:17 (KJV)

A friend loveth at all times, and a brother

is born for adversity.

6. Proverbs 22:24 (KJV)

*Make no friendship with an angry man;
and with a furious man thou shalt not go:*

7. Proverbs 27:17 (KJV)

*Iron sharpeneth iron; so a man
sharpeneth the countenance of his friend.*

8. Luke 11:5 (KJV)

*And he said unto them, Which of you shall
have a friend, and shall go unto him at
midnight, and say unto him, Friend, lend
me three loaves;*

9. John 15:13 (KJV)

Greater love hath no man than this, that a man lay down his life for his friends.

ACKNOWLEGDEMENTS

To my leadership: Thank you for your prayers, believing in me, spiritual guidance, encouragement, and wisdom. To share with other friends and individuals the importance of using their faith, following leadership, and prayer for the Kingdom of God. To my family and friends for your love and support. God as brought me over many tribulations, and studying the Word of God, I have gained a closer relationship with Him. Without Jesus being my Lord and Savior of my life, this book would not exist. As we continue to grow together, God will always be first, taking us higher in him. Glory to God! Hallelujah!

About the Author

It been S. A. Polk passion and desire to have a closer relationship with God. To share her book with other friends and individuals on the importance of using their faith and knowing how to get answers from every time they pray. She is blessed to have many friends in Christ. She prays that everyone who reads this book will draw closer to Christ and become a partner to get the gospel out into all the world.

ShonBooks.com

Notes

Made in the USA
Columbia, SC
06 March 2022